The Mystery
of the
Poisoned
Pudding

Written by Josh Lacey

Illustrated by Jim Field

Published by Pearson Education Limited, Edinburgh Gate, Harlow, Essex, CM20 2JE
Registered company number: 872828

www.pearsonschools.co.uk

Text © Josh Lacey 2011

Designed by Bigtop
Original illustrations © Pearson Education 2011
Illustrated by Jim Field

The right of Josh Lacey to be identified as author of this work has been asserted
by him in accordance with the Copyright, Designs and Patents Act 1988.

First published 2011

15 14 13 12
10 9 8 7 6 5 4 3

British Library Cataloguing in Publication Data

A catalogue record for this book is available from the British Library

ISBN 978 1 408 27383 8

Printed and bound in Malaysia, CTP-VP

Acknowledgements
We would like to thank the children and teachers of Bangor Central Integrated
Primary School, NI; Bishop Henderson C of E Primary School, Somerset;
Brookside Community Primary School, Somerset; Cheddington Combined School,
Buckinghamshire; Cofton Primary School, Birmingham; Dair House Independent
School, Buckinghamshire; Deal Parochial School, Kent; Newbold Riverside Primary
School, Rugby and Windmill Primary School, Oxford for their invaluable help in
the development and trialling of the Bug Club resources.

Every effort has been made to contact copyright holders of material reproduced
in this book. Any omissions will be rectified in subsequent printings if notice is
given to the publishers.

Contents

This is the story of an expensive restaurant and an enormous meal and a poisoned pudding, but all those things come later. Before anything else, it's the story of a boy named Matt Clarke who couldn't speak French.

He didn't even want to speak French. Given the choice, he would just have spoken English. But he wasn't given the choice. He was only eleven years old and his parents made those kinds of decisions for him.

This is what they decided. That summer, Matt would spend two weeks with a girl named Véronique. First, she would stay with him for a week in England and speak nothing but English. (If you want to find out what happened, you can read about it in *The Mystery of the Missing Finger*.)

Then Matt would travel to France and stay with Véronique's family, speaking nothing but French. After a fortnight, each of them would be fluent in the other's language.

That was the idea, anyway.

This evening was Matt's first in France. He was having supper at a restaurant named Pamplemousse, which belonged to Véronique's father, Gustav Petit. The three of them were sitting together at a table in the middle of the restaurant. (Véronique's mother died a long time ago and her father had never married again.)

Every couple of minutes, someone
different would come to the table and
say hello to Monsieur Petit, or ask him a
question. Whoever they were – waiters,
chefs, diners or friends – they all spoke in
French.

Matt tried to understand what they were
saying. Once or twice, he even tried to say
a few French words himself, but they all
spoke so fast that his ears couldn't keep up,
let alone his mouth.

Left to himself, he spent most of the meal looking around the restaurant, staring at the paintings on the walls and watching the other diners. He found his attention drawn again and again to an enormously fat man sitting alone at a little table in a dimly lit corner near the door to the kitchen. He was eating his way slowly through an apparently endless meal, seemingly relishing every mouthful.

The man had started his meal with a bowl of small brown snails in their small brown shells. Matt had never seen anyone eat a snail before, so he watched carefully as the man dug inside each shell with a long fork, pulling out a squishy lump of snail and popping it into his mouth.

A waiter took away the bowl of empty shells and returned a few minutes later with a plate of a dozen oysters. When the fat man had dispatched them down his throat, the waiter brought a whole lobster to the table, accompanied by a large bowl of fresh mayonnaise. Next came a small joint of lamb, then a thick steak smothered in creamy sauce. So much food would have filled up most people, but this man wanted even more.

He ordered a chocolate pudding served on a large white plate. Smiling happily to himself, he wiped his silver spoon carefully on his thick linen napkin, dipped it delicately into the pudding and transferred a tiny sliver to his mouth. He swallowed, licked his lips and reached for another spoonful.

Then his face changed colour.

His cheeks went red. His eyes opened a little wider. A yellow froth appeared around his mouth, dribbling out of his lips and dripping onto his white shirt.

Matt watched in amazement, wondering what was happening.

The fat man put his hands on the table and tried to push himself to his feet, but all the strength seemed to have drained from his body. Helplessly, he sank back into his chair and shivered slightly as if he had just felt a cold breeze blowing down the back of his neck. Then he toppled forwards and fell nose-first into his pudding.

Matt panicked. I have to help, he thought. But what can I do?

He looked around the packed, noisy restaurant, wondering if anyone else had noticed, but all the other diners were too engrossed in their own dinners and their own conversations.

Matt hissed across the table, "Véronique, look at that man! We've got to help him!"

"*En français*," commanded Véronique. "You must speak only in French!"

"Not now, Véronique! This is serious!" Matt pointed at the fat man. "I think he's dead!"

Realising that Matt wasn't joking, Véronique turned to see who he was pointing at. When she saw the diner face-down in his pudding, she immediately grabbed her father's sleeve and cried, "Papa!"

Gustav Petit rushed to the fat man's side, followed by Véronique and Matt. Together, the three of them eased him from his chair and lowered him to the ground.

A dab of chocolate remained fixed to his nose. Yellow froth dribbled from his mouth. He was breathing unsteadily and his face had turned an unusual shade of green.

Gustav stood up and called out, "*Il y a un docteur ici?*"

The restaurant suddenly went quiet, and everyone turned to see what the fuss was about.

Then a man jumped to his feet. He was a doctor who happened to be dining in Pamplemousse with his family. He knelt on the floor, took one look at the fat man and ordered Gustav to ring 112. (That's the emergency number in France.) The doctor muttered something in French in a low voice. Matt didn't understand what he said, but he did understand the look of shock on the faces of Véronique and her father.

Luckily an ambulance reached the restaurant within minutes and the police followed swiftly afterwards.

By this time, the kitchen was in chaos. The dining-room too. Only the hungriest people were still eating. Most of the diners, the waiters, the chefs, even the boy who did the washing-up, were crowding round the man on the floor, wondering if he would live or die.

The paramedics pushed their way through the crowd, loaded their patient into their ambulance and drove him to hospital, sirens wailing. Meanwhile, the police ordered the chefs to stop cooking and the diners to stop eating. They suspected that the fat man had been poisoned.

Gustav Petit was sitting alone, biting his nails and worrying about the consequences. His restaurant would have to remain closed until the police had discovered if the mysterious fat man really had been poisoned, who had done it, how and – most importantly – why. That might take weeks or even months. During that time, the chefs and the waiters would have to sit at home, twiddling their thumbs, doing nothing, and not a single meal would be served. Even worse, what would happen to the restaurant's reputation? When Pamplemousse eventually reopened, would anyone ever want to eat there again?

17

"*C'est un désastre*," said Véronique, watching her father with sad eyes. "Papa has worked all his life for this place. Now – pfff! – it is all gone. And there is nothing we can do."

"There is one thing," said Matt. "We could find the poisoner ourselves."

"Us? How?"

"We found the thief at Marchmont Hall."

"Ah, but this is different."

"Why?"

"There is no thief here. This is *un grand problème* in the restaurant, Mathieu. There is a bad oyster, perhaps, or some bad meat, and it gives stomach trouble – how you say, food poisoning? – to the person who eats it."

"That's not what happened here," said Matt. "This man was poisoned deliberately – and the poison was in the chocolate pudding."

"How do you know?"

"Because I saw what happened. I was watching the man right from the start of his meal. I saw him eat his way through the snails, the oysters, the lobster, the lamb and the steak – and he didn't have any problems at all. He was fine till he took the first mouthful of the chocolate pudding. Then he suddenly got this yellow froth around his mouth and collapsed face-first onto the table. This isn't an ordinary case of food poisoning, Véronique. Someone tried to kill this man."

For a moment, Véronique didn't say a word. She just thought about what Matt had said. Then she smiled. "You are right, Mathieu. You and me – we will find the truth and save Pamplemousse for Papa! Where do we start?"

"With the chocolate pudding," said Matt. "Do you know who made it?"

"*Bien sûr*. Here, all the chocolate dishes are made by one man – Albert Noisette."

"Then we have to talk to him."

Albert Noisette was sitting alone in the kitchen, dreaming about chocolate.

He was the restaurant's chief chocolatier. He created all the chocolate dishes that were eaten in Pamplemousse. Chocolate cakes and chocolate puddings and chocolate soufflés and chocolate éclairs – all of them were made by Albert Noisette. When he went home at night, his skin smelled of chocolate, and when he lay in bed, he dreamed about chocolate, and when he woke up in the morning, he started thinking about new things to make with chocolate.

"*Bon soir*, Albert," said a familiar voice.

Albert looked up.

He saw the boss's daughter and a boy he didn't know. Véronique introduced him as her English friend, Mathieu.

Véronique had some questions for Albert. He didn't really feel like chatting, but he answered them as well as he could. He spoke in French and Véronique translated his answers.

Véronique asked Albert about the chocolate pudding. She wanted to know how he had made it, where the ingredients had come from and, most importantly, if anyone could have tampered with the pudding before it was taken from the kitchen to the diner at his table in the restaurant.

Albert shook his head. Chocolate was his whole life, so he was very careful about his ingredients. He had his own cupboard and fridge, with locks on the doors.

"Ask him if someone could have picked any of the locks," said Matt. "What if someone opened the cupboard or the fridge and added some poison to the chocolate before he started making the pudding?"

Véronique translated the question for Albert, who shook his head.

"*C'est impossible*," he said, explaining that only he had the keys and he would have noticed if anyone had tampered with one of the locks. Also, he always tasted his own creations. If the pudding had been poisoned, he would have been very ill too, but he felt fine.

"Ask him who else could have touched the pudding," said Matt. "Could anyone have added poison to it while Albert was making it? Had he left the kitchen or turned his back at any point, even for a moment?"

Albert gave a simple answer: "*Non.*"

"Can you ask him one more question?" said Matt. "After he made the pudding and before the fat man ate his first mouthful, could anyone else have touched it?"

"*Seulement les deux*," said Albert. Only two people could have touched the pudding. The first was his assistant, Marie-Claire, who had carried the pudding from Albert's table to the counter at the end of the kitchen. The second was Pierre, the waiter, who had taken the pudding from the counter into the restaurant and delivered it to the diner.

Matt listened carefully to Véronique's translation. Then he said, "We'd better talk to Marie-Claire and Pierre."

Outside the restaurant, a local TV camera crew had set up their equipment for a live broadcast, while some journalists snapped photographs and yelled questions. They had all had a tip-off that someone had been poisoned. By tomorrow morning, news of the poisoning would have spread, and Pamplemousse would be famous – for all the wrong reasons.

The police cordoned off the entrance with tape, allowing no one to enter or leave.

They told the press that the inspector who had been brought in to investigate the case would soon be making an official statement.

Inside the restaurant, Inspecteur Alain Timbre was supervising operations. Some of his officers were taking the details of anyone who had been eating or working in Pamplemousse that evening. Others were securing all the food on the premises. Everything in the kitchen, and all the uneaten food in the dining-room, would be packed up and taken to the police laboratories for analysis.

The restaurant was gradually emptying out. Once the diners had given their details to the police, they were allowed to leave.

On an ordinary evening, Gustav Petit would have made sure that the children got back home safely after dinner, even if he had to stay behind to carry on working at the restaurant. This evening, however, Véronique and Matt were left to look after themselves. Which suited them very well. They had things to do too.

They searched through the restaurant and the kitchen until they found a small woman with pale skin and dark eyes. This was Marie-Claire Madeleine, Albert's assistant. She worked with him on all his creations, making chocolate soufflés and chocolate cakes and chocolate bonbons and chocolate ice-creams and chocolate sauces and every other type of chocolate that anyone might want to eat in the restaurant. Now, still wearing her white apron covered with splashes of chocolate, she was sitting alone at a table, sipping a cup of camomile tea, waiting to be allowed to go home.

Marie-Claire seemed perfectly happy to talk to Véronique and Matt, but she didn't tell them anything that they didn't already know. Tonight, she explained, she had helped Albert create the chocolate pudding for the diner, fetching ingredients and stirring the mixture, and she was sure that no one could have tampered with it.

Once the pudding was ready, she had put it on a white plate, placed it in Pierre's hands and watched him carry it out to the dining-room. Until that moment, Marie-Claire said, the pudding had never left her sight. Apart from Albert, Pierre and herself, no one else could have touched it.

Véronique and Matt thanked Marie-Claire and went to find Pierre.

Down at the far end of the kitchen, three men were sitting at a table, playing cards. All of them were waiters and now they were waiting to go home.

Pierre was winning. He didn't want to leave the table, especially not to talk to two kids. But Véronique was the boss's daughter, so he reluctantly agreed to answer her questions.

"*Deux minutes*," he said.

He put his cards on the table and joined Matt and Véronique in a quiet corner.

Véronique asked him the same questions that she had asked Albert and Marie-Claire. Pierre gave his answers in short sentences or single words, "*oui*" or "*non*", confirming everything that they had already heard from Albert and Marie-Claire.

"Between the moment that he picked up the pudding," said Matt, "and the moment that he delivered it to the diner, could anyone have done anything to it?"

Véronique translated the question and Pierre answered in French, saying that he had only been holding the pudding for thirty or forty seconds. During that time, the pudding had never left his hands and no one else could possibly have touched it.

After Pierre had gone back to his game, Matt and Véronique talked in whispers, discussing what they had gleaned from talking to Albert, Marie-Claire and Pierre.

From their vantage point, they could look around the kitchen and see all three of their suspects: Albert, sitting alone, dreaming about chocolate, Marie-Claire sipping tea, and Pierre playing cards.

"One of them has to be guilty," said Matt. "The only question is, which one?"

"*C'est impossible*," said Véronique.

"What do you mean? What's impossible?"

"I know Albert, Marie-Claire and Pierre. All of them, they work for my father for many years. They are not liars."

"They're the only people who had access to the pudding. One of them must have poisoned it. That's the only explanation."

"Perhaps you are wrong," suggested Véronique. "Maybe someone else is guilty. Or no one."

"What's that supposed to mean? How could no one be guilty?"

"Maybe he poison the pudding himself."

"You think the fat man poisoned his own pudding?"

"It is possible – no?"

"Why?"

"Think about it, Mathieu! Maybe the fat man, he is very unhappy."

"You mean suicide?" Matt thought for a moment. Then he shook his head. "I was watching him the whole time and I'm sure he didn't put anything in the pudding. As soon as it was placed in front of him, he picked up his spoon and started eating."

"Then perhaps the oyster is poisoned," suggested Véronique. "Or the lamb, or the steak. Perhaps it is a poison that takes some time to work."

"No, it was definitely the chocolate that poisoned him," said Matt. "As soon as he swallowed the first mouthful, he got sick. The poison couldn't have been in anything else."

"Oh, I don't know, Mathieu!" Véronique put her head in her hands. "It is hopeless!"

For a little while, Véronique had really believed that she and Matt might be able to solve the case by finding out who had poisoned the fat man and prevent her father's restaurant from going bankrupt, but now she was losing hope.

Matt wished he could console her, but he didn't know what to say or do. He began to feel a bit guilty. Perhaps he shouldn't even have suggested they try to solve the 'mystery of the poisoned pudding' themselves. Perhaps they should just leave everything to the police. After all, he and Véronique were just a couple of kids. How could they possibly think they could solve a crime like this? They needed clues, and there didn't seem to be any.

They sat in silence for a moment.

"Motive!" said Matt suddenly.

Véronique looked at him. "*Quoi*?"

"Motive," repeated Matt. "It's obvious that either Albert or Marie-Claire or Pierre must have poisoned the pudding. The only question is, which one of them? Whoever it was, they must have had a motive. You don't poison someone without a good reason. Which of them had a good enough reason for poisoning the fat man?"

Véronique didn't answer. She just shrugged her shoulders.

Matt knew it was going to be difficult to convince Véronique that one of her father's trusted staff must be guilty.

"How about Albert?" asked Matt. "What do you know about him? Could he be a poisoner?"

Véronique shook her head. "Albert, he cares about only one thing. Chocolate. Here, he is very happy, because he can spend all day working with chocolate."

"What about Pierre? What does he care about?"

"Money," said Véronique. "Pierre, he loves money. He would maybe kill someone for their money."

"That's interesting. Maybe someone paid him to poison the fat man. And what about Marie-Claire? What does she love?"

"Ah, Marie-Claire." Véronique shook her head sadly from side to side. "She has a very sad story."

"What happened to her?"

"Some years ago, she is a super chef. People come to her restaurant from all over France. They love her food. Everyone is saying she will be a great chef. And then, one day, a newspaper publish a review of her restaurant. The review says she is no good. Her food is no good. Her restaurant is no good. Everything is no good. After that review, no one will ever eat in her restaurant again. And so she must get a job as an assistant, here in Pamplemousse."

Matt thought for a moment. "Who wrote the review?" he asked.

Véronique shrugged her shoulders. "I don't know."

"Have you got a computer here?"

"Yes. It is in Papa's office. *Pourquoi*?"

"I'll tell you in a minute. Come on!"

Matt and Véronique sneaked into Gustav Petit's office and closed the door quietly.

Matt switched on the computer and Véronique keyed in the words: Marie-Claire Madeleine Restaurant Review (in French, of course).

The response came back immediately. At the top of the results was a review written several years ago by a food critic called Emmanuel Blanc, describing a visit to Marie-Claire's restaurant. Véronique read the first few lines of the review and shook her head slowly from side to side.

"*Terrible*," she said.

"What's so *terrible*?" asked Matt.

"What this man says about poor Marie-Claire and her restaurant – it is *terrible*."

Inspecteur Timbre was standing by the entrance to the kitchen, discussing with Gustav Petit the date that Pamplemousse might be allowed to open again. They were so involved in their discussion that neither of them noticed as two figures walked quietly through the dining-room and stopped beside them.

Matt cleared his throat and said, "*Excusez-moi?*"

Neither man appeared to hear him.

"I know what happened," said Matt, speaking a little louder.

Still they took no notice.

If he had been alone, Matt might just have gone away, not wanting to cause too much fuss, and come back later when the inspector wasn't in the middle of a heated discussion. But he couldn't just sneak away while Véronique was watching him. He'd feel like an idiot. So he cleared his throat and spoke even louder. "Inspector? Um, hello, Inspector? Actually, I think I know what happened."

Still no response.

That was when Véronique got involved. "Papa!" she snapped in a loud voice.

Gustav Petit smiled wearily at his daughter. "*Oui, ma chérie*?" Then he noticed Matt. "Ah, Mathieu, hello. I am very sorry about this *catastrophe*. You will excuse me, I hope, but I must talk with the *inspecteur*. Véronique will take you home."

"I have to talk to the inspector myself," said Matt.

"You do?" Gustav Petit was surprised. "About what?"

"I need to know the name of the man who was poisoned."

The inspector shook his head. "I cannot tell you," he said. "This is only for the police to know. Not for boys and girls."

"Is it Emmanuel Blanc?" asked Matt.

The inspector was astonished. "How do you know that?"

As soon as Marie-Claire was confronted by the police, she confessed everything.

She had been waiting for this moment for years, she said. Ever since Gustav Petit gave her a job, in fact, she had been carrying a vial of poison in her handbag, waiting for the day that Emmanuel Blanc might come to eat in Pamplemousse. When he wrote his terrible review of her own restaurant, he destroyed her career and her life and she was determined to get her revenge on him.

She knew how Emmanuel Blanc worked: he always visited a new restaurant as a mystery diner, so that he could eat his way through the menu without anyone knowing who he was. He didn't want to be given special treatment by the kitchen or the waiters. No one knew what he looked like – there was never a photo of him with his reviews. But Marie-Claire had been determined to track him down, and she had succeeded. That was why she was able to identify him when he came into Pamplemousse. This was her chance! Just before handing the chocolate pudding to Pierre, she tipped the poison over it ...

The police led her away in handcuffs and
Inspecteur Timbre allowed Gustav Petit to
reopen his restaurant immediately.

The next evening, there was a huge celebration in Pamplemousse. Gustav Petit threw a party for his chefs, his waiters, his most loyal customers and everyone else connected with the restaurant.

Matt and Véronique sat together at the head of a long table. People kept coming up to them and offering their congratulations. Without them, the restaurant wouldn't have reopened for days, weeks or even months. They had saved everyone's jobs – and Pamplemousse itself.

To celebrate, the head chef served them with a special dinner, starting with a plate of snails.

Matt had never eaten a snail before.

"Don't worry," said Véronique, pushing the big white plate towards him. "She is delicious."

"She?" said Matt, gingerly picking up one of the six small brown snails sitting in the middle of the plate. "How do you know it's a she?"

Véronique just laughed. "Come on," she said, "you have to try *un escargot*. It is delicious."

Matt stared for a moment at the snail he was holding between his fingers, imagining the squishy flesh inside the shell, then popped the whole thing into his mouth.

He chewed nervously.

To his surprise, the snail tasted rather like chocolate.

In fact, it tasted exactly like chocolate.

He was just about to ask Véronique whether all snails taste like chocolate or just this one, when he noticed three people standing around the table, watching him: Gustav Petit, Albert and Pierre. They were laughing.

That afternoon, they had discussed a special pudding to celebrate the reopening of Pamplemousse, and Albert had set to work to create one. Matt was the first person to try it.

"You like it?" asked Véronique.

"I love it!" said Matt, and he reached for another chocolate snail.